ALSO EDITED BY WILLIAM COLE
The Fireside Book of Humorous Poetry
Eight Lines and Under

* *PITH*
& VINEGAR

AN ANTHOLOGY OF SHORT HUMOROUS POETRY
EDITED BY

* *WILLIAM COLE*

SIMON AND SCHUSTER • NEW YORK

FIRST PRINTING

SBN 671–20362–2
LIBRARY OF CONGRESS CATALOG CARD NUMBER: 75–84119
MANUFACTURED IN THE UNITED STATES OF AMERICA BY AMERICAN BOOK—STRATFORD PRESS, INC.
NEW YORK, N.Y.

ACKNOWLEDGMENTS

*For arrangements made with various authors, their representatives, and publishing houses
where copyrighted material was permitted to be reprinted, and for the courtesy extended by
them, the following acknowledgments are gratefully made. All possible care has been taken
to trace the ownership of every selection included and to make full acknowledgment for its
use. If any errors have accidentally occurred, they will be corrected in subsequent editions,
provided notification is sent to the publisher.*

Fadiman Associates, Ltd., for "Alimentary" and "Theological" by Clifton Fadiman; copyright © 1956 by The New Yorker Magazine, Inc.
The New Yorker Magazine for "Testing, Testing" by Dan Dillon, reprinted by permission;
copyright © 1940, 1968 by The New Yorker Magazine, Inc.
The New Yorker Magazine for "Midsummer Melancholy" by Margaret Fishback, reprinted by permission; copyright © 1927, 1955 by Margaret Fishback; originally in *The
New Yorker*.
The New Yorker Magazine for "Geography: A Song" by Howard Moss, reprinted by per-
mission; © 1968 by The New Yorker Magazine, Inc.
The New Yorker Magazine for "Vacation Trip" by William Stafford, reprinted by per-
mission; © 1968 by The New Yorker Magazine, Inc.
The New Yorker Magazine for "Episode of the Cherry Tree" by Mildred Weston, re-
printed by permission; copyright © 1932, 1960 by The New Yorker Magazine, Inc.
George Allen & Unwin Ltd. for a clerihew from *Bank Holiday on Parnassus* by Allan M.
Laing, copyright by Allan M. Laing.
Kingsley Amis for "Terrible Beauty" from *A Look Round the Estate*, published by Jona-
than Cape 1967; copyright © 1967 by Kingsley Amis.
Appleton-Century-Crofts for "Bringing Him Up" by Lord Dunsany from *Number Four
Joy Street*, Mabel Marlowe, editor. Reprinted by permission of Appleton-Century-Crofts.
Atheneum Publishers for double dactyls by Sally Belfrage, Anthony Hecht, John Hol-
lander, Paul Pascal, and E. William Seaman, from *Jiggery Pokery*, edited by Anthony
Hecht and John Hollander. Copyright © 1966 by Anthony Hecht and John Hollander. Re-
printed by permission of Atheneum Publishers.
The Atlantic Monthly Company for "Sidewalk Orgy" by Richard O'Connell; copyright
© 1967 by The Atlantic Monthly Company, Boston, Mass. Reprinted by permission.
Robert Bly for "Ducks"; reprinted by permission of the author.
Jonathan Cape Ltd. for "Banana" by Adrian Mitchell from *Out Loud*, published by
Cape Goliard Press and, in America, by Grossman Publishers. Reprinted by permission.
Chatto and Windus Ltd. for "Lines for an Eminent Poet and Critic" from *The Scale of
Things*, by Patric Dickinson. Reprinted by permission.
Clarke, Irwin & Company Ltd. for "The Loneliness of the Long Distance Runner" from
Bread, Wine and Salt, by Alden Nowlan; published by Clarke, Irwin & Company Ltd. Re-
printed by permission.
Victor Contoski for "Invitation"; first published by *Quixote* magazine.
Collins-Knowlton-Wing, Inc. for "Twins," copyright © 1968 by Robert Graves; re-
printed by permission of Collins-Knowlton-Wing, Inc.
Constable Publishers for "Wishes of an Elderly Man" from *Laughter from a Cloud* by
Lady Raleigh. Reprinted by permission.
Hilary Corke for "The Snake."

(continued on page 155)

✳ *CONTENTS*

✳ *INTRODUCTION*

The only other collection of epigrammatic verse published in this century was put together in 1928 by an Englishman named George Rostrevor Hamilton. He called it, logically enough, *The Soul of Wit*. Hamilton was a pretty stuffy bird, and in his Introduction he boasts of having eliminated certain poems that were of "a distressing species of vulgarity." He obviously did not agree with his contemporary, Logan Pearsall Smith, who said that "An improper mind is a perpetual feast." However, even without vulgarities, Hamilton's book had some fine and funny things, and I have looted it shamelessly.

An epigram is defined in one dictionary as "a short poem leading up to and ending in a witty or ingenious turn of thought." The word comes from the Greek *epigramma*, which has to do with an inscription carved on a monument. Such monument inscriptions evolved into pithy rhymed comments, many quite vinegary, which were gathered together in the first poetry anthology, known as *The Greek Anthology*, in about 60 B.C. The poems I've collected here are not all epigrams. Some are short flights of sheer nonsense, some are proper little lyric poems, others are specialized verse forms. There are three kinds of poems I haven't used: limericks, haiku, and what I call "nothing poems." We have by now had a surfeit of limericks. The vulgar ones are fine for sniggering boys, but that bump bumpety bumpety bump bump becomes terribly monotonous. Haiku are about as amusing as the Japanese themselves. And a "nothing poem" is the kind of jingle that appeared on the "Post Script" page of the late unlamented *Saturday Evening Post,* or in the currently lamentable *Look:* rhymed platitudes about domestic situations or life's minor inconveniences.

As you will see, the masters of terse verse are Hilaire Belloc, Ogden Nash, W. H. Auden, and J. V. Cunningham. It is interesting (and annoying) that the two greatest masters of light verse, W. S. Gilbert and C. S. Calverley, who were contemporaries in nineteenth-century England, wrote absolutely nothing that would fit within the twelve-line limit I've set for this collection. Nor did my favorite neglected contemporary humorous poet, Wallace Irwin. They don't even excerpt well.

I have uncovered most of these poems through dogged, though delightful, research. Others have been plucked from a mind that resembles a pack rat's nest. But with typical pack rat carelessness, I find that there are two couplets left over whose authors I can't remember or locate. I've asked those who should know, and they don't. Dear Reader (a phrase I've always wanted to use), can you tell me who wrote:

Do you love me or do you not?
You told me once but I forgot.

In an earlier anthology for children, I attributed it to Anonymous, but I'm sure there's an author lurking around somewhere.

The other puzzler is:

My soul is dark with stormy riot,
Directly traceable to diet.

There they are, pithy and vinegary enough; short but not sweet. But who wrote them? I'd like to know.

WILLIAM COLE

It is not foolish all, nor is it wise all,
Nor is it true in all, nor is it lies all.
JONATHAN SWIFT

I *
WORD PLAYS
&
TRICKY FORMS

✳ Geography: A Song

There are no rocks
At Rockaway,
There are no sheep
At Sheepshead Bay,
There's nothing new
In Newfoundland,
And silent is
Long Island Sound.

HOWARD MOSS

✳ Hallelujah!

"Hallelujah!" was the only observation
That escaped Lieutenant-Colonel Mary Jane,
When she tumbled off the platform in the station,
And was cut in little pieces by the train.
    Mary Jane, the train is through yer:
    Hallelujah, Hallelujah!
We shall gather up the fragments that remain.

A.E. HOUSMAN

✳ THE LAMA

The one-l lama,
He's a priest.
The two-l llama,
He's a beast.
And I will bet
A silk pajama
There isn't any
Three-l lllama.*

OGDEN NASH

✳ MIDSUMMER MELANCHOLY

Oh, somewhere there are people who
Have nothing in the world to do
But sit upon the Pyrenees
And use the very special breeze
Provided for the people who
Have nothing in the world to do
But sit upon the Pyrenees
And use the . . .

MARGARET FISHBACK

* The author's attention has been called to a type of conflagration known as a three-alarmer. Pooh!

✳ An Aristocratic Trio

'Mongst illustrious men in the Bible there be
King Domcome, Lord Howlong, and Baron Fig-tree.
     JUDSON FRANCE

✳ Garlic

Garlic's taste is briefest pleasure—
Eat in haste, repent at leisure.
Garlic's like the poor, like sorrow—
Here today and here tomorrow.
     JUSTIN RICHARDSON

✳ A Bird in the Bush

I live in hope some day to see
The crimson-necked phalarope;
 (Or do I, rather, live in hope
To see the red-necked phalarope?)
     LORD KENNET

✳ A Thousand Hairy Savages

A thousand hairy savages
Sitting down to lunch
Gobble gobble glup glup
Munch munch munch.

SPIKE MILLIGAN

✳ Testing, Testing

Now is the time for all good men
To come from the hills, the woods, and the glen.
To come to the aid of the quick brown fox,
The quick little, slick little smarty.
To come to the aid of the pretty little fox,
To come to the aid of their party.

DAN DILLON

✳ The Purist

I give you now Professor Twist,
A conscientious scientist.
Trustees exclaim, "He never bungles!"
And send him off to distant jungles.
Camped on a tropic riverside,
One day he missed his loving bride.
She had, the guide informed him later,
Been eaten by an alligator.
Professor Twist could not but smile.
"You mean," he said, "a crocodile."

OGDEN NASH

✳ Red Wine

With fish, which always is served first,
White wine may slake the urgent thirst.
Red wine, however, we postpone—
The nearer the sweet, the meeter the Beaune.

JUSTIN RICHARDSON

✳ SELECTIONS FROM
QUAKE, QUAKE, QUAKE:
A LEADEN TREASURY OF
ENGLISH VERSE

O nuclear wind, when wilt thou blow
    That the small rain down can rain?
Christ, that my love were in my arms
    And I had my arms again.

✳

We buried him darkly at dead of night
    And his corpse to the ramparts we hurried.
A flashburn is not an agreeable sight
    And the Other Ranks might have got
        worried.

✳

Jack and Jill went up the hill
    To fetch some heavy water.
They mixed it with the dairy milk
    And killed my youngest daughter.

*

Flight-Sergeant Foster flattened Gloucester
    In a shower of rain.
(A Mr. Hutton had pressed the wrong button
    On the coast of Maine.)

*

In a cavern, in a canyon
    Lay an unexpected mine.
Don't know where, dear. DO TAKE CARE, DEAR . . .
    Dreadful sorry, Clementine.

*

Hark, the herald angels sing
    Glory to the newborn thing
Which, because of radiation
    Will be cared for by the nation.
        PAUL DEHN

* INGENIOUS RACONTEUR

Last autumn's chestnuts, rather *passées,*
He now presents as *marrons glacées.*
        RENÉE HAYNES

✳ In Roman

Hate and debate Rome through the world hath spread,
Yet *Roma amor* is, if backward read.
    Then is't not strange Rome hate should foster? No:
    For out of backward love, all hate doth grow.
        SIR JOHN HARINGTON (1561–1612)

✳ A Child That Has a Cold

A child that has a cold we may suppose
Like wintry weather—Why?—it blows *its nose*.
        THOMAS DIBDIN (1771–1841)

✳ My Invention

Guess what I have gone and done;
I've invented a light that plugs into the sun.
    For the sun is bright enough,
    And the bulb is strong enough—
        But the cord isn't long enough.
        SHEL SILVERSTEIN

A Concrete Poem

miniskirtminiskirt
miniskirtminiskirtmi
niskirtminiskirtminisk
irtminiskirtminiskirtmin

leglegleglegleglegleg leglegleglegleglegleg

shoe shoe

ANTHONY MUNDY

The pronunciation of Erse
Gets worse and worse;
They spell it Cuchulain—
No fuchulain!

A. D. HOPE

✳ EPITAPH ON A MARF*

Wot a marf 'e'd got,
Wot a marf.
When 'e was a kid,
Goo' Lor' luv'll
'Is pore old muvver
Must 'a' fed 'im wiv a shuvvle.

Wot a gap 'e'd got,
Pore Chap,
'E'd never been known to larf,
'Cos if 'e did
It's a penny to a quid
'E'd 'a' split 'is fice in 'arf.
ANONYMOUS

✳

O you chorus of indolent reviewers,
Irresponsible, indolent reviewers,
Look, I come to the test, a tiny poem
All composed in the metre of Catullus . . .
Hard, hard, hard is it, only not to tumble,
So fantastical is the dainty metre.
ALFRED, LORD TENNYSON

* Marf: Cockney, "mouth"

✻ TRIOLET

"I love you, my Lord!"
    Was all that she said—
What a dissonant chord,
    "I love you, my Lord!"
Ah! how I abhorred
    That sarcastic maid!—
"I love you? My *Lord!"*
    Was all that she said.
                    PAUL T. GILBERT

✻ A CUBIC TRIOLET

```
T H I S T R I O L E T
I S L I T T L E F U N
S O H A R D T O G E T
T H I S T R I O L E T
I N F U N A N D Y E T
E X A C T L Y D O N E
T H I S T R I O L E T
I S L I T T L E F U N
```
          ANONYMOUS

∗ DOUBLE DACTYLS

The double dactyl is a verse form invented by Anthony Hecht and Paul Pascal in 1951, and featured in a book, Jiggery Pokery, *edited by Mr. Hecht and fellow-poet John Hollander in 1967. Here is how the editors describe the form:*

"The form . . . is composed of two quatrains, of which the last line of the first rhymes with the last line of the second. All the lines except the rhyming ones, which are truncated, are composed of two dactylic feet. The first line of the poem must be a double dactylic nonsense line, like 'Higgledy-piggledy,' or 'Pocketa-pocketa.' . . . The second line must be a double dactylic name. And then, somewhere in the poem, though preferably in the second stanza, and ideally in the antepenultimate line, there must be at least one double dactylic line that is one word long. . . ."

Although the form is strict, the inventors raised no fuss and brought no suit when George Starbuck rang in changes, some examples of which you will find at the end of these selections.

✳ DANISH WIT

Higgledy-piggledy
Franklin D. Roosevelt
High over Jutland flew
In from the East;

"Well," quipped a Minister
Plenipotentiary,
"*Something* is Groton in
Denmark, at least!"

JOHN HOLLANDER

✳ LAST WORDS

"Higgledy-piggledy
Andrea Doria
Lives in the name of this
Glorious boat.

As I sit writing these
Non-navigational
Verses a—CRASH! BANG! BLURP!
GLUB" . . . (end of quote).

JOHN HOLLANDER

✳ THE LOWER CRITICISM

Higgledy-piggledy
Dorothy Richardson
Wrote a huge book with her
Delicate muse.

Where (though I hate to seem
Uncomplimentary)
Nothing much happens and
Nobody screws.

JOHN HOLLANDER

✳ WRATH

Higgledy-piggledy
Ludwig van Beethoven
Scornful of cheer, and of
Hearing forlorn,

Spitefully hissing, sat
Writing unplayable
Pianississississimo
Notes for the horn.

JOHN HOLLANDER

✳

Higgledy-piggledy
Ludwig van Beethoven
Bored by requests for some
Music to hum,

Finally answered with
Oversimplicity,
"Here's my Fifth Symphony:
Duh, duh, duh, DUM!"

E. WILLIAM SEAMAN

✳ FIRMNESS

Higgledy-piggledy
Mme. de Maintenon
Shouted, "Up yours!" when ap-
Proached for the rent,

And, in her anger, pro-
Ceeded to demonstrate,
Iconographically,
Just what she meant.

ANTHONY HECHT

✳ Tact

Patty-cake, patty-cake,
Marcus Antonius
What do you think of the
African Queen?

Gubernatorial
Duties require my
Presence in Egypt. Ya
Know what I mean?

PAUL PASCAL

✳ Progress

Higgledy-piggledy
Thomas A. Edison
Turned on a switch with a
Wave of his wand,

Giving his name to some
Organizational
Chaps in whose light we are
Now being Conned.

SALLY BELFRAGE

✳ Poor Kid

Higamus hogamus
Gloria Vanderbilt
Said to her husband, "I've
Terrible luck!

Acting and poetry,
Painting and book reviews,
Multidiversity—
Can't make a buck!"

WILLIAM COLE

✳ Geeandess

Niminy piminy
Gilbert and Sullivan
Collaborated and
Got very rich.

Nevertheless (though quite
Characteristically)
Each thought the other
A bit of a twitch.

WILLIAM COLE

✳

Albany schmalbany
Governor W.
Averell Harriman
Served but a term.

Ambassadorial
Potentialities
Beckoned, and so did the
Harriman firm.
GEORGE STARBUCK

✳

Jiminy Whillikers
Admiral Samuel
Eliot Morison,
Where is your ship?

"I am the H. M. S.
Historiography's
Disciplinarian.
Button your lip!"
GEORGE STARBUCK

✳

Clippety cloppity
Cesare* Borgia
Modeled himself on his
Father the Pope:

Pontifex maximus,
Paterfamilias,
Generalissimo:
He was no dope.

GEORGE STARBUCK

✳ SAID

President Johnson to
Harrison Salisbury,
"Czechoslovakia?
Blankety-blank.

Blankety-blankety-
Blankety. Blankety?
Blankety-blankety-
Blankety-blank."

GEORGE STARBUCK

* The Borgias were a Spanish-Italian family. In this case we prefer the tri-syllabic pronunciation of "Cesare," as in Spanish.

✳ SAID

Agatha Christie to
E. Phillips Oppenheim,
"Who is this Hemingway?
Who is this Proust?

Who is this Vladimir
Whatchamacallum, this
Neopostrealist
Rabble?" she groused.

GEORGE STARBUCK

✳ SAID

J. Alfred Prufrock to
Hugh Selwyn Mauberly:
"Whatever happened to
Senlin? Ought-nine."

"One with a passion for
Orientalia?"
"Rather." "Lost track of him."
"Pity." "Design."

GEORGE STARBUCK

✳ *CLERIHEWS*

The clerihew was invented by the English writer Edmund Clerihew Bentley (1875–1956) when he was sixteen. Clerihews are usually biographical in nature and consist of two rhyming couplets. There are no restrictions concerning the length of the lines.

✳

Edmund Clerihew Bentley,
Looking at his name one day intently,
Found that it contained that very new
Verse form, the clerihew.

WILLIAM JAY SMITH

✳ Some Clerihews by Bentley

The Art of Biography
Is different from Geography.
Geography is about Maps,
But Biography is about Chaps.

Sir Christopher Wren
Said, "I am going to dine with some men.
If anybody calls
Say I am designing St. Paul's."

George the Third
Ought never to have occurred.
One can only wonder
At so grotesque a blunder.

The great Emperor Otto
Could not decide upon a motto.
His mind wavered between
L'Etat C'est Moi and *Ich Dien.*

Geoffrey Chaucer
Took a bath (in a saucer)
In consequence of certain hints
Dropped by the Black Prince.

"Susaddah!" exclaimed Ibsen,
"By dose is turdig cribson!
I'd better dot kiss you.
Atishoo! Atishoo!"

The digestion of Milton
Was unequal to Stilton.
He was only feeling so-so
When he wrote *Il Penseroso.*

✳

Diodorus Siculus
Made himself ridiculous.
He thought a thimble
Was the phallic symbol.
ANONYMOUS

✳

Albert Dürer
Naturally never heard of the Führer.
I wonder if the latter . . .?
But that doesn't really matter.
W. LESLIE NICHOLLS

✳ ALIMENTARY

The herbivorous Thoreau
Would emerge from his pondside burrow
Whenever he grew thinner,
And walk over to the Emersons' for a
      chicken dinner.
CLIFTON FADIMAN

✳ THEOLOGICAL

Said Descartes, "I extol
Myself because I have a soul
And beasts do not." (Of *course*
He *had* to put Descartes before the horse.)

      CLIFTON FADIMAN

William Penn
Was the most level-headed of men;
He had only one mania—
Pennsylvania.

      WILLIAM JAY SMITH

The Empress Poppaea
Was really rather a dear,
Only no one could stop her
From being improper.

      ANONYMOUS

The Saturday Review
Has little to do
With literature as such,
Or with anything very much.
WILLIAM COLE

Instead of blushing cherry hue
at having invented the clerihew,
Mr. E. C. Bentley
just smiles gently.
ALLAN M. LAING

II *
REAL
&
IMAGINARY
PEOPLE

❋ The Taste of Space

McLuhan put his telescope to his ear;
What a lovely smell, he said, we have here.

A. J. M. SMITH

❋ On Noman, a Guest

Dear Mr. Noman, does it ever strike you
That the more we see of you, the less we like you?

HILAIRE BELLOC

❋ The Devil's Walk

From his brimstone bed at the break of day,
A-walking the Devil has gone,
To visit his snug little farm of the earth,
And see how his stock goes on.
Over the hill and over the dale,
He walked, and over the plain:
And backward and forward he swished his long tail,
As a gentleman swishes his cane.

ROBERT SOUTHEY (1774–1843)

✳ On Sir Henry Ferrett, M.P.

"Seeing is believing,"
I've often heard you say.
My dear Sir Henry Ferrett,
I see you every day.

> "BEACHCOMBER"
> (J. B. MORTON)

✳ Lines on a Certain Friend's Remarkable Faculty for Swift Generalization

"How do you do?" Will asked of me.
"Very well, thanks," said I. Said he,
"Yes, I invariably find
Abundant health in all mankind."

Next morning, "How d'you do?" asked Will.
I said that I was rather ill.
"Alas," his voice toll'd like a bell,
"Mankind was ever far from well."

> MAX BEERBOHM

✻ Addressed to a Gentleman at Table, Who Kept Boasting of the Company He Kept

What of lords and dukes with whom you have supped,
  And dukes and lords that you dined with yestreen!
A louse, sir, is still but a louse,
  Though it crawl on the locks of a queen.
    ROBERT BURNS (1756–1796)

✻ On Dr. Lettsom, by Himself

When people's ill, they come to I,
  I physics, bleeds, and sweats 'em;
Sometimes they live, sometimes they die.
  What's that to I? I lets 'em.
    JOHN COAKLEY LETTSOM
    (1744–1815)

✳ DIRGE

Just at the blackest bit of my depression
    Somebody somewhere tunes a clarinet,
Scrapes up a chair to start a scrabble session,
    Elopes or gets a raise or wins a bet.
I find it perfectly infuriating
    That when I'm in the depths of my despair
Somebody somewhere starts off celebrating.
    It makes one wonder if they really *care*.
       HAZEL TOWNSON

✳ BRINGING HIM UP

(to be read solemnly)

Mister Thomas Jones
Said to James, his son:
"Never swallow bones,
Never point a gun.

Never slam a door,
Never play with flames,
Never shun the poor."
"Dull old fool!" said James.
       LORD DUNSANY

✳ LINES FROM CROTCHET CASTLE

He took castle and towns; he cut short limbs and lives;
He made orphans and widows of children and wives;
This course many years he triumphantly ran,
And did mischief enough to be called a great man.
THOMAS LOVE PEACOCK (1785–1866)

✳ TWINS

Siamese twins: one, maddened by
The other's moral bigotry,
Resolved at length to misbehave
And drank them both into the grave.
ROBERT GRAVES

✳ THE SKEPTIC

My Father Christmas passed away
When I was barely seven.
At twenty-one, alack-a-day,
I lost my hope of heaven.

Yet not in either lies the curse;
The hell of it's because
I don't know which loss hurt the worse—
My God or Santa Claus.
ROBERT SERVICE

✳ To Someone Who Insisted
I Look Up Someone

I rang them up, while touring Timbuctoo,
Those bosom chums to whom you're known as "Who?"
X. J. KENNEDY

✳ To The Noble Woman of
Llanarth Hall

(*Who shut the Author's goat in a house for two days, its crime being that it grazed too near the Mansion*)

O black-maned, horse-haired, unworthy one,
    What did you do to the goat, your sister?
She'd your father's horns, your mother's beard—
    Why did you put her falsely in prison?
EVAN THOMAS (1710?–1770?)
Translated from the Welsh by Anthony Conran

✳ On a Politician

How richly, with ridiculous display,
The Politician's corpse was laid away.
While all of his acquaintance sneered and slanged,
I wept: for I had longed to see him hanged.
HILAIRE BELLOC

✳ MENDAX

See yonder goes old Mendax, telling lies
To that good easy man with whom he's walking;
How know I that? you ask, with some surprise;
Why, don't you see, my friend, the fellow's talking.

> ANONYMOUS
> *From the German of Gotthold Lessing* (1729–1781)

✳ ON TWO MINISTERS OF STATE

Lump says that Caliban's of gutter breed,
And Caliban says Lump's a fool indeed,
And Caliban, and Lump and I are all agreed.

> HILAIRE BELLOC

✳ ON A CERTAIN LORD GIVING SOME THOUSAND POUNDS FOR A HOUSE

So many thousands for a house
For you, of all the world, Lord Mouse!
A little house would best accord
With you, my very little lord!
And then exactly matched would be
Your house and hospitality.

> DAVID GARRICK (1716–1779)

✳ PROFESSOR DRINKING WINE

The oboes on the terrace held a chord
and died away to silence, Clitheroe poured—
bored—still more brandy for the moon-faced priest;
the moon hung rusty in the clouded east.
Oboe and harpsichord, more slow and high,
began the adagio. "Eighteen children die
for want of food in India at each chord,"
thought Clitheroe, with precision, as he poured.

ALASDAIR CLAYRE

✳ AT NEWMARKET

See on Newmarket's turf, my lord
    Instructs his jockey how to trim;
Who, to make sure of full reward,
    First cheats all round—and then cheats him.
How similar parts extremes assume!
Like groom, like peer! like peer, like groom!

SAMUEL BISHOP (1731–1895)

✳ EPIGRAM

This is my curse, *Pompous,* I pray
That you believe the things you say
And that you live them, day by day.

J. V. CUNNINGHAM

❋ DOCTOR EMMANUEL

Doctor Emmanuel Harrison-Hyde
Has a very big head with brains inside.
I wonder what happens inside the brains
That Doctor Emmanuel's head contains.

JAMES REEVES

❋ THE CURSE

*To a sister of an enemy of the author's who disapproved of
"The Playboy"*

Lord, confound this surly sister,
Blight her brow with blotch and blister,
Cramp her larynx, lung, and liver,
In her guts a galling give her.

Let her live to earn her dinners
In Mountjoy with seedy sinners:
Lord, this judgment quickly bring,
And I'm your servant, J. M. Synge.

JOHN MILLINGTON SYNGE

I've labored long and hard for bread—
For honor and for riches—
But on my corns too long you've tread
You fine-haired sons of bitches.

      BLACK BART*

✳ FROM HUMBUG RHYMES

Fishing for sticklebacks, with rod and line,
    Goes Ebeneza Isac Walton, junior,
His age is just a little under nine,
    If he be more than that he's rather puny, or
If he be less than that, and only five,
    Then he's the finest boy I've ever seen alive.

      SIR FRANCIS BURNAND

* Around 1880 a stagecoach robber known as Black Bart was traced
and captured through the laundry mark on a dropped handkerchief.
He was a mild, elderly character fond of leaving his poetry at the
scene of his crime.

✳ TONY O

Over the bleak and barren snow
A voice there came a-calling:
"Where are you going to, Tony O!
Where are you going this morning?"

"I am going where there are rivers of wine,
The mountains bread and honey;
There Kings and Queens do mind the swine,
And the poor have all the money."

COLIN FRANCIS

✳ A SERIOUS DANGER

Sylla declares the world shall know
That he's my most determined foe!
I wish him wide the tale to spread;
For all that I from Sylla dread
Is, that the knave, to serve some end,
May one day swear that he's my friend.

R. A. DAVENPORT (1777?–1852)

✳ A Foren Ruler

He says, *My reign is peace,* so slays
    A thousand in the dead of night.
Are you all happy now? he says,
    And those he leaves behind cry *Quite.*
He swears he will have no contention,
    And sets all nations by the ears;
He shouts aloud, *No intervention!*
    Invades, and drowns them all in tears.
      WALTER SAVAGE LANDOR (1775–1864)

✳ On a Lord

Here lies the Devil—ask no other name.
Well—but you mean Lord ———? Hush! We mean
    the same.
      SAMUEL TAYLOR COLERIDGE (1772–1834)

✳ On Andrew Turner

In se'enteen hunder an' forty-nine,
Satan took stuff to mak' a swine,
    And cuist it in a corner;
But wilily he chang'd his plan,
And shaped it something like a man,
    And ca'd it Andrew Turner.
      ROBERT BURNS

✳ To a Rogue

Thy beard and head are of a different dye:
Short of one foot, distorted in an eye:
With all these tokens of a knave complete,
Should'st thou be honest, thou'rt a dev'lish cheat.

JOSEPH ADDISON (1672–1719)
(Imitated from Martial)

✳ Spaniel's Sermon

'Tis more than Spaniel's place is worth
To speak his masters ill;
As long as there is Peace on Earth
He teaches men goodwill.

But when the shells begin to fly
He calls our quarrel just
And bids us keep our powder dry
And place our God in trust.

COLIN ELLIS

III *
POETS
&
CRITICS

❋ A Rhymester

Jem writes his verses with more speed
    Than the printer's boy can set 'em;
Quite as fast as we can read,
    And only not so fast as we forget 'em.

SAMUEL TAYLOR COLERIDGE

❋ A Caution to Poets

What poets feel not, when they make,
    A pleasure in creating,
The world, in *its* turn, will not take
    Pleasure in contemplating.

MATTHEW ARNOLD (1822–1888)

✳ THE BARDS

My aged friend, Miss Wilkinson,
　　Whose mother was a Lambe,
Saw Wordsworth once, and Coleridge, too,
　　One morning in her pram.

Birdlike the bards stooped over her
　　Like fledgling in a nest;
And Wordsworth said, "Thou harmless babe!"
　　And Coleridge was impressed.

The pretty thing gazed up and smiled,
　　And softly murmured, "Coo!"
William was then aged sixty-four
　　And Samuel sixty-two.

　　　　WALTER DE LA MARE

✳ THE NAUGHTY PREPOSITION

I lately lost a preposition;
　　It hid, I thought, beneath my chair.
And angrily I cried: "Perdition!
　　Up from out of in under there!"

Correctness is my vade mecum,
　　And straggling phrases I abhor;
And yet I wondered: "What should he come
　　Up from out of in under for?"

　　　　MORRIS BISHOP

✽ Lines for an Eminent Poet and Critic

He has come to such a pitch
Of self-consciousness that he
Dare not scratch, if he has the **itch,**
For fear he is the flea.

PATRIC DICKINSON

✽ Lecture Note: Elizabethan Period

He wrote a final poem down. Then died
Before the liquid shining on the three last letters dried.
It fluttered from his table to the floor
Where kittens played with it while daughters cried.
For days it lay in fluff and dust behind the door.
A maid then picked it up, to have the solar
Tidy for the funeral bakes, and dropped it in the **jakes,**
So fate had him and all the rest of us well bitten.
Now irretrievably beshitten it was, dear sirs,
The one immortal poem he had written.

GEOFFREY GRIGSON

✳ TO CRITICS

I'll write, because I'll give
You Critics means to live;
For should I not supply
The Cause, the Effect would die.

ROBERT HERRICK (1591–1674)

✳ THE POET'S FATE

What is the modern Poet's fate?
To write his thoughts upon a slate;
The Critic spits on what is done,
Gives it a wipe—and all is gone.

THOMAS HOOD (1799–1845)

✳ VARIATIONS ON A THEME BY WILLIAM CARLOS WILLIAMS

1

I chopped down the house that you had been saving
    to live in next summer.
I am sorry, but it was morning, and I had nothing to do
and its wooden beams were so inviting.

2

We laughed at the hollyhocks together
and then I sprayed them with lye.
Forgive me. I simply do not know what I am doing.

3

I gave away the money that you had been saving to
    live on for the next ten years.
The man who asked for it was shabby
and the firm March wind on the porch was so juicy and cold.

4

Last evening we went dancing and I broke your leg.
Forgive me. I was clumsy, and
I wanted you here in the wards, where I am a doctor!

KENNETH KOCH

✳ Telegram One

TO: COYMISTRESS
FROM: MARVELL

INTERNALLY EXTERNALLY ENTIRELY
ETERNALLY
MARVELBODY WOULD JUMP PROYOU
BUT
TIMEBUGGED CHARIOTED TOMBWARDS STOP
SO UNCOY SOONEST ANDY
      ADRIAN MITCHELL

✳ The Envious Critick

The Poor in Wit or Judgement, like all Poor,
Revile, for having least, those who have more:
So, 'tis the Critick's Scarcity of Wit
Makes him traduce them who have most of it.
Since to their Pitch himself he cannot raise,
He them to his mean Level would debase.
Acting like Demons, that would All deprive
Of Heav'n, to which themselves can ne'er arrive.
      WILLIAM WYCHERLEY (1640–1716)

✳ Visiting Poet

"The famous bard, he comes! The vision nears!"
Now heaven protect your booze. Your wife. Your ears.
              JOHN FREDERICK NIMS

✳ Literary Zodiac

"Behind the man the writer moles away."
—The London *Sunday Times* on H. E. Bates

The writer tenebrously moles away;
He beavers at his manuscript all day;
Occasionally he'll sloth awhile and brood
Before (or after) pythoning some food.
His publisher gorillas when he's heard
The author tortoises from word to word;
The agent squirrels at the long delay.
While the tax gatherer spiders for his prey.
              R. A. PIDDINGTON

✳

No teacher I of boys or smaller fry,
No teacher I of teachers, no, not I.
Mine was the distant aim, the longer reach,
To teach men how to teach men how to teach.
              ALLEN BEVILLE RAMSAY (1872–1955)

✳ SPECIALIST

If the compass of his mind
Matched his Renaissance behind
He could range like Paracelsus
Through his field and someone else's.

THEODORE ROETHKE

✳ MISS SNOOKS, POETESS

Miss Snooks was really awfully nice
And never wrote a poem
That was not really awfully nice
And fitted to a woman.

She therefore made no enemies
And gave no sad surprises
But went on being awfully nice
And took a lot of prizes.

STEVIE SMITH

✻ Now We Are Sick

Hush, hush,
Nobody cares!
Christopher Robin
Has
   Fallen
      Down-
         Stairs.
      "Beachcomber"
       (J. B. MORTON)

✻ On Thomas Hood

Jealous, I own it, I was once,
That wickedness I here renounce.
I tried at wit . . . it would not do . . .
At tenderness . . . that failed me too,
Before me on each path there stood
The witty and the tender Hood.
      WALTER SAVAGE LANDOR

✳ MENDING SUMP

"Hiram, I think the sump is backing up.
The bathroom floor boards for above two weeks
Have seemed soaked through. A little bird, I think,
Has wandered in the pipes, and all's gone wrong."
"Something there is that doesn't hump a sump,"
He said; and through his head he saw a cloud
That seemed to twinkle. "Hiram, well," she said,
"Smith is come home! I saw his face just now
While looking through your head. He's come to die
Or else to laugh, for hay is dried-up grass
When you're alone." He rose, and sniffed the air.
"We'd better leave him in the sump," he said.

KENNETH KOCH

✳ TO A POET, WHO WOULD HAVE
ME PRAISE CERTAIN BAD POETS,
IMITATORS OF HIS AND MINE

You say, as I have often given tongue
In praise of what another's said or sung,
'Twere politic to do the like by these;
But was there ever dog that praised his fleas?

WILLIAM BUTLER YEATS

✳ ON THE IMPRINT OF THE FIRST ENGLISH EDITION OF THE WORKS OF MAX BEERBOHM

"London: JOHN LANE, *The Bodley Head*
 New York: CHARLES SCRIBNER'S SONS."
This plain announcement, nicely read,
  Iambically runs.

MAX BEERBOHM

✳ TO THE POET T. J. MATHIAS

The Piper's music fills the street,
The Piper's music makes the heat
  Hotter by ten degrees:
Hand us a Sonnet, dear Mathias,
Hand us a Sonnet cool and dry as
  Your very best, and we shall freeze.

WALTER SAVAGE LANDOR

IV *
HERE LIES

✳ At Leeds

Here lies my wife,
    Here lies she;
Hallelujah!
    Hallelujee!
        FROM *Norfolk's Epitaphs,* 1861

✳ On John Adams, of Southwell

John Adams lies here, of the parish of Southwell,
A Carrier who carried his can to his mouth well:
He carried so much, and he carried so fast,
He could carry no more—so was carried at last;
For, the liquor he drank, being too much for one,
He could not carry off, so now he's carri-on.
      GEORGE GORDON, LORD BYRON (1788–1824)

✳ On an Insignificant Fellow

Colley fell ill, and is no more!
His fate you bid me to deplore;
But what the deuce is to be said?
Colley was living, Colley's dead.
        LORD CURZON OF KEDLESTON

Epitaph

To the Four Husbands of
Miss Ivy Saunders
1790, 1794, 1808, 18?

Here lie my husbands One Two Three
    Dumb as men could ever be
As for my fourth well praise be God
    He bides a little above the sod
        Alex Ben Sandy were the
        First three names
        And to make things tidy
        I'll add his—James

✳ Epitaph on a Career Woman

She was generous, helpful, went out of her way
    For anyone well connected;
She was noted for doing good deeds in the dark
    In hopes that they'd be detected.
      WILLIAM COLE

✳

    Wha lies here?
I, Johnny Dow.
Hoo! Johnny, is that you?
Ay, man, but a'm dead now.
      ANONYMOUS

❋ On a Bookseller

Here lies poor Ned Pardon, from misery freed,
Who long was a bookseller's hack;
He led such a damnable life in this world,
I don't think he'll ever come back.

OLIVER GOLDSMITH (1731–1774)

❋ Paddy Murphy

The night that Paddy Murphy died
I never shall forget!
The whole damn town got stinking drunk
And they're not sober yet.

There is one thing they did that night
That filled me full of fear:
They took the ice right off the corpse
And stuck it in the beer.

That's how they showed their respect for
    Paddy Murphy,
That's how they showed their honor and their
    fight,
That's how they showed their respect for
    Paddy Murphy
They drank his health in ice-cold beer that
    night!

ANONYMOUS

✳ On a Royal Demise

How monarchs die is easily explained,
    And thus it might upon the tomb be chiseled,
"As long as George the Fourth could reign
        he reigned,
    And then he mizzled."
        THOMAS HOOD

✳ Epitaph on a Warthog

Now death has sealed my warthog's eyes,
And in this narrow grave he lies.
His "double," I am glad to say,
Delights us yet, as Lady A——.
        "Beachcomber"
        (J. B. MORTON)

✳ Lines on the Author's Death

*Written with the Supposed View of Being Handed to
Rankine after the Poet's Interment*

He who of Rankine sang, lies stiff and dead,
And a green grassy hillock hides his head;
Alas! alas! a devilish change indeed!
        ROBERT BURNS

✳ On Sir John Vanbrugh, Architect

Under this stone, reader, survey
Dear Sir John Vanbrugh's house of clay.
Lie heavy on him, earth! for he
Laid many heavy loads on thee.

ABEL EVANS (1679–1737)

✳ Epitaph

After reading Ronsard's lines from Rabelais

If fruits are fed on any beast
Let vine-roots suck this parish priest,
For while he lived, no summer sun
Went up but he'd a bottle done,
And in the starlight beer and stout
Kept his waistcoat bulging out.

Then Death that changes happy things
Damned his soul to water springs.

JOHN MILLINGTON SYNGE

V *
LOVE IS

✳ LOVE

is the unexpected ring of the Cancer
Society lady on an endless Sunday afternoon
when no one's supposed to be home. You put down
your section of the *Times* and shuffle to the door
and open it a crack, leaving the chain on:
"You're on my list!" she says, with a smile
that makes you feel ashamed to feel so well.
"I'm sorry, I already gave," you answer,
knowing, as you say it, that this is one
who won't take no.

GERALD JONAS

✳ SWEET, LET ME GO!

Sweet, let me go! Sweet, let me go!
What do you mean to vex me so?
Cease, cease, cease your pleading force!
Do you think thus to extort remorse?
Now, now! no more! alas, you overbear me;
And I would cry, but some would hear, I fear me.

ANONYMOUS
(*seventeenth century*)

✻ I Thought I Saw Stars

I thought I saw stars, when first I saw your eyes,
So luminous they were, and such an enormous size;
I fell on the floor and foamed at the mouth, with
     inconsequential cries.

Now, when I look in your eyes, I do not flinch;
Heaven forgive me, I am not even tempted to lynch
The men who, standing beside you, display an inclination
     to pinch.

For this insensitivity may I be pardoned.
I looked in your eyes too often, and in the end became
     hardened;
There came a day when Adam turned his back upon Eve,
     and gardened.

           R. P. LISTER

✳ MARY ANN

He's bought a bed and a table too,
A big tin dish for making stew,
A large flat-iron to iron his shirt,
And a flannel, and a scrubbing brush to wash away
    the dirt.
And he's brought a pail and basins three,
A coffee pot, a kettle, and a teapot for the tea,
    And a soap-bowl and a ladle,
    And a gridiron and a cradle,
And he's going to marry Mary Ann, that's me!
He's going to marry Mary Ann!

      JOSEPH TABRAR
       (*nineteenth century*)

✳ LILAC TIME

The lilacs are flowering, sweet and sublime
  with a perfume that goes to the head;
and lovers meander, in prose and in rhyme
trying to say
    for the thousandth time—
    what's easier done than said.

      PIET HEIN

❋ Responsibility

'Tis easy enough to be twenty-one:
'Tis easy enough to marry;
But when you try both games at once
'Tis a bloody big load to carry.

ANONYMOUS

❋ To Ianthe

You smiled, you spoke, and I believed,
By every word and smile deceived.
Another man would hope no more;
Nor hope I what I hoped before:
But let not this last wish be vain;
Deceive, deceive me once again!

WALTER SAVAGE LANDOR

❋ Token

I love you more than the gilder his gilding
        and more than the dove his dove
and more than all the people in the Wool-
        worth Building
        love all the people they love.

PEGGY BACON

✳ WERE YOU ON THE MOUNTAIN?

O, were you on the mountain, or saw you my love?
Or saw you my own one, my queen and my dove?
Or saw you the maiden with the step firm and free?
And say, is she pining in sorrow like me?

I was upon the mountain, and saw there your love,
I saw there your own one, your queen and your dove;
I saw there the maiden with the step firm and free,
And she was *not* pining in sorrow like thee.

Translated from the Irish
by DOUGLAS HYDE

✻ THE NEWLYWEDS

After a one-day honeymoon, the Fishers rushed off to a soft drink bottlers' convention, then to a ball game, a TV rehearsal and a movie preview.—Life

"We're married," said Eddie.
Said Debbie, "Incredi-

ble! When is our honey-
moon?" "Over and done," he

replied. "Feeling logy?
Drink Coke," "Look at Yogi

go!" Debbie cried. "Groovy!"
"Rehearsal?" "The movie."

"Some weddie," said Debbie.
Said Eddie, "Yeah, mebbe."
                    JOHN UPDIKE

*

There was a strife 'twixt man and maid—
Oh that was at the birth of time!
But what befell 'twixt man and maid,
Oh that's beyond the grip of rhyme.
'Twas, "Sweet, I must not bide with you,"
And, "Love, I cannot bide alone";
For both were young and both were true,
And both were hard as the nether stone.

RUDYARD KIPLING

* Memoir

We loved: we vowed our love should never die.
Who was she? For that matter, who was I?

R. G. HOWARTH

VI *

SEX

&

SUCH

❋ "Tomorrow Is Saint Valentine's Day"

Tomorrow is Saint Valentine's day,
    All in the morning betimes,
And I a maid at your window,
    To be your Valentine.

Then up he rose, and donn'd his clothes,
    And dupp'd* the chamber door;
Let in the maid, that out a maid
    Never departed more.
                WILLIAM SHAKESPEARE (1564–1616)

❋ Apologia

I may be fast, I may be loose,
I may be easy to seduce,
I may not be particular
To keep the perpendicular,
Not all my horizontal friends
Are princes, peers, and reverends,
When Tom or Dick or Bertie call
They leave me strictly vertical.
                HERBERT FARJEON

* *dupp'd:* opened up

✳ EURYNOME

Come all old maids that are squeamish
And afraid to make mistakes,
Don't clutter your lives up with boyfriends:
The nicest girls marry snakes.

If you don't mind slime on your pillow
And caresses as gliding as ice
—Cold skin, warm heart, remember,
And besides, they keep down the mice—

If you're really serious-minded,
It's the best advice you can take:
No rumpling, no sweating, no nonsense,
Oh who would not sleep with a snake?

       JAY MACPHERSON

✳ SIDEWALK ORGY

When I see her walk before me
               I am seized
By a desire to assault her all
At once as Zeus zoomed down on naked Leda.

Unfortunately I am not a swan
Nor would she understand my reference.

       RICHARD O'CONNELL

✳ Epigram

Good Fortune, when I hailed her recently,
Passed by me with the intimacy of shame
As one that in the dark had handled me
And could no longer recollect my name.

J. V. CUNNINGHAM

✳ Dinah

Some are too difficult to win.
I work to remove her doubt.
By the time I've figured me in,
She's already figured me out.

A. R. AMMONS

✻ MISUNDERSTANDING

I placed
my hand
upon
her thigh.

By the way
she moved
away
I could see
her devotion
to literature
was not
perfect.

IRVING LAYTON

✻ THE BEDBUG

Comrade, with your finger on the playback switch,
Listen carefully to each love-moan,
And enter in the file which cry is real, and which
A mere performance for your microphone.

TONY HARRISON

✶ To Cloe

Cloe's the wonder of her sex,
    'Tis well her heart is tender;
How might such killing eyes perplex,
    With virtue to defend her!

But Nature, graciously inclined,
    Not but to vex but please us,
Has to her boundless beauty joined
    A boundless will to ease us.
      GEORGE GRANVILLE, LORD LANSDOWNE (1667–1735)

✶

Lip was a man who used his head.
He used it when he went to bed
With his friend's wife, and with his friend,
With either sex at either end.
    J. V. CUNNINGHAM

✳ RIDDLE

I'm a strange creature, for I satisfy women,
a service to the neighbors! No one suffers
at my hands except for my slayer.
I grow very tall, erect in a bed,
I'm hairy underneath. From time to time
a beautiful girl, the brave daughter
of some churl dares to hold me,
grips my russet skin, robs me of my head
and puts me in the pantry. Presently that girl
with plaited hair who has confined me
Remembers our meeting. Her eyes moisten.

Translated from the Old English
by KEVIN CROSSLEY-HOLLAND

✳ ONCE, TWICE, THRICE

Once, twice, thrice, I Julia tried,
The scornful puss as oft denied,
And since I can no better thrive,
I'll cringe to ne'er a bitch alive.
So kiss my Arse, disdainful sow!
Good claret is my mistress now.

SEVENTEENTH-CENTURY ENGLISH CATCH

✳ HOSTIA

This one deceives her husband with her eyes,
And this one with a thousand proper lies;
Hostia, such is her regard for me,
Deceives me not at all but lets me see
The queer bites on her voluptuous thighs,
IRVING LAYTON

✳

Busts and bosoms have I known
    Of various shapes and sizes,
From grievous disappointments
    To jubilant surprises.
ANONYMOUS

✳ A TOAST

Here's to you and here's to me,
And here's to the girl with the well-shaped knee.
Here's to the man with his hand on her garter;
He hasn't got far yet, but he's a damn good starter.
ANONYMOUS

✷ STAND, STATELY TAVIE

Stand, stately Tavie, out of the codpiece rise,
And dig a grave between thy Mrs. Thighs;
Swift stand, then stab 'til she replies,
Then gently weep, and after weeping, die.
Stand, Tavie, and gain thy credit lost;
Or by this hand I'll never draw thee, but against a post.

SEVENTEENTH-CENTURY ENGLISH SONG

✷ EPIGRAM

Dear, my familiar hand in love's own gesture
Gives irresponsive absence flesh and vesture.

J. V. CUNNINGHAM

✷

Spring is hard on us;
Summer in bed we muss;
Fall the exploding beast;
Winter, post-coital triste.

ANONYMOUS (*twentieth century*)

✷ TERRIBLE BEAUTY

Hearing how tourists, dazed with reverence,
Look through sun-glasses at the Parthenon,
I thought of that cold night outside the Gents
When Dai touched Gweneth up with his gloves on.

KINGSLEY AMIS

✳ To Scilla

Storm not, brave Friend, that thou hast never yet
Mistress nor Wife that others did not swive,
But, like a Christian, pardon and forget,
For thy own Pox will they Revenge contrive.

SIR CHARLES SEDLEY (1639?–1701)

✳ The Snake

She was seated of her goodness on my knee
And under her dress, but talking of fodder and flocks,
I had slipped, in a casual voice of good dogs,
My hand.

Her legs were warm and firm.

"There is a snake," she said, "under my dress." Then
I said: "I know. I am looking for it."

HILARY CORKE

*

I was in Vegas. Celibate and able
I left the silver dollars on the table
And tried the show. The black-out, baggy pants,
Of course, and then this answer to romance:
Her ass twitching as if it had the fits,
Her gold crotch grinding, her athletic tits,
One clock, the other counter-clockwise twirling.
It was enough to stop a man from girling.

J. V. CUNNINGHAM

* NYMPHS AND SATYRS

The satyr's mouth is stained red with wine,
The nymph is beautifully white.
The nymph is resisting—all very fine—
The satyr is slightly tight.

But it isn't exactly as you think
For here's a remarkable matter:
The inside of the nymph is as wet and pink
As the lustful lips of the satyr.

GAVIN EWART

✻

I saw your hinee
cha cha cha
It's bright and shinee
cha cha cha
If you don't hide it
cha cha cha
I'm gonna bide it
cha cha cha
         ANONYMOUS *(seven years old)*

VII *
WIVES
&
OTHERS

❋ THE VOICE OF EXPERIENCE

Meet women with tender bearing,
you will conquer them, I bet;
and the quick man who is daring
will perhaps do better yet;
but the man who seems uncaring
what response he may unloose
will offend and thus seduce.

JOHANN WOLFGANG VON GOETHE (1749–1832)
*Translated from the German
by Walter Kaufman*

❋ OF WOMEN

Woman: that is to say
A body which the birds of prey
Disdain to take away.

Woman: the word implies
A thing which lies
With you at night, about you at sunrise.

Translated from The Arabian Nights
by E. Powys Mathers

✳ THE LONELINESS OF THE LONG DISTANCE RUNNER

My wife bursts into the room
where I'm writing well
of my love for her

and because now
the poem is lost

I silently curse her.

ALDEN NOWLAN

✳ COLOR BLIND

How shocking the stocking that matches the pink
    Of the lip, or the tip of the nose, or the rose!
How vile on the nylon the blue shadows blink!
    How rank on the ankle the weedy green grows!

How sickly the thickly-set calf in its tint
    Of mauve or of clover; its strawberry mesh!
What on *earth* could give birth to the horrible hint
    That has made us afraid of the shade of the flesh?

CAROL PAINE

✳ VACATION TRIP

The loudest sound in our car
was Mother being glum:

> little chiding valves,
> a surge of detergent oil,
> all that deep chaos,
> the relentless accurate fire,
> the drive shaft wild to arrive,

and, tugging along behind in its great big balloon,
that looming piece of her mind—

"I wish I hadn't come."
                    WILLIAM STAFFORD

✳ A WIFE

Lord Erskine, at women presuming to rail,
Calls a wife "a tin canister tied to one's tail";
And fair Lady Anne, while the subject he carries on,
Seems hurt at his Lordship's degrading comparison.
But wherefore degrading? considered aright,
A canister's useful, and polished, and bright:
And should dirt its original purity hide,
That's the fault of the puppy to whom it is tied.
                    M. G. LEWIS (1775–1818)

❋ HIGH-LIFE LOW-DOWN

To his Castle Lord Fothergay bore his young bride,
And he carried her over the drawbridge so wide,
Through the Great Hall, the Solar, the West Hall, the East,
And thirty-eight principal bedrooms at least,
Up seventeen stairways and down many more
To a basement twelve yards by a hundred and four,
And at last set her down—he was panting a bit—
In front of the sink and said, "Kid, this is IT."

JUSTIN RICHARDSON

❋ NOT LATE ENOUGH

When you are late and have not let me know,
I see you falling under squealing wheels,
Or battling blindly through the piling snow,
Or running with a ruffian at your heels . . .
Dramatic scenes which instantly convert
My wrath into an all-forgiving woe
That lasts until you stagger home unhurt,
Gabbling wild lies of ruffians, skids or snow.

HAZEL TOWNSON

✱ On Lady Poltagrue, a Public Peril

The Devil, having nothing else to do,
Went off to tempt My Lady Poltagrue.
My Lady, tempted by a private whim,
To his extreme annoyance, tempted him.

HILAIRE BELLOC

✱ The Bulge

Nobody knows what's growing in Bridget,
    Nobody knows whose is, what's more:
Maybe a beauty queen, maybe a midget,
    Maybe a braided bloke to stand by the door.

Lovely full Bridget, her eyes are figs,
    Her belly's an ocean, heaving with fish,
Her heart is a barnyard with chickens and pigs,
    Her outside's a banquet, her tongue is a dish.

Something enormous is bulging in Bridget—
    A milkman, a postman, a sugar-stick, a slop,
An old maid, a bad maid, a doughhead, a fidget.
    Multiple sweet Bridget, what will she drop?

GEORGE JOHNSTON

✳ Evening in the Suburbs

At the segregated party
I remember my position.
I move in among the women.
Only fast girls brave the censure
Of the watching married women.
Only they go to the men's group.
How I wish that I dare join them—
Hear the sharp and funny stories,
Drink my fill the way the men do—
I am stranded at the blunt end
Where the new is all domestic
And the drinks are Lilliputian.

STELLA BARNETT

✳ I Cannot Wash My Eye Without an Eyecup

I cannot wash my eye without an eyecup,
Its shape is such that nothing else will do;
One time I tried it with a towel,
It almost made me cry;
One time I tried it with a toothbrush;
And I darn near lost my eye.

I cannot wash my eye without an eyecup,
To find this out ten dear, long years it took,
And if it were not for my scruples,
I'd go 'round with filthy pupils,
Giving everyone I know a dirty look.

AMERICAN COLLEGE SONG

✳ On the Inconstancy of Women: From the Latin of Catullus

My fair says, she no spouse but me
Would wed, though Jove himself were he,
    She says it: but I deem
That what the fair to lovers swear
Should be inscribed upon the air,
    Or in the running stream.

GEORGE LAMB

✽ REUNION

I cannot call you as lovely as you were,
    After so many years; nor shall I try.
Look what has happened to your skin, eyes, hair!
      You are *much* uglier . . . and so am I.
        PAUL DEHN

✽ TRIOLET

All women born are so perverse
No man need boast their love possessing.
If nought seem better, nothing's worse:
All women born are so perverse.
From Adam's wife, that proved a curse
Though God had made her for a blessing,
All women born are so perverse
No man need boast their love possessing.
      ROBERT BRIDGES

✽ FAIR, RICH, AND YOUNG

Fair, rich, and young: how rare is her perfection,
Were it not mingled with one foul infection!
I mean, so proud a heart, so curst a tongue,
As makes her seem nor fair, nor rich, nor young.
    SIR JOHN HARINGTON (1561–1612)

✳ A REFLECTION

When Eve upon the first of Men
     The apple pressed with specious cant,
O, what a thousand pities then
     That Adam was not Adamant.
         THOMAS HOOD

✳ IT'S NO GOOD!

It's no good, the women are in eruption,
and those that have been good so far
now begin to steam ominously,
and if they're over forty-five, hurl great stones
     into the air
which are very like to hit you on the head as you
     sit
on the very slopes of the matrimonial mountain
where you've sat peacefully all these years.

Vengeance is mine, saith the Lord,
but the women are my favorite vessels of wrath.
         D. H. LAWRENCE

VIII *
THE NATURE
OF THINGS

✳

Pick a quarrel, go to war,
Leave the hero in the bar;
Hunt the lion, climb the peak:
No one guesses you are weak.
W. H. AUDEN

✳ THE EMPLOYMENTS OF LIFE

Through all the employments of life
Each neighbor abuses his brother;
Trull and rogue they call husband and wife:
All professions berogue one another.

For the priest calls the lawyer a cheat,
The lawyer beknaves the divine;
And the statesman, because he's so great,
Thinks his trade as honest as mine.
JOHN GAY (1685–1732)

✳ FAME

Ten thousand flakes about my window blow,
Some falling and some rising, but all snow.
Scribblers and statesmen! are ye not just so?
WALTER SAVAGE LANDOR

✳ THE WORLD

The world is a well-furnished table,
    Where guests are promiscuously set:
We all fare as well as we're able,
    And scramble for what we can get.
        THOMAS LOVE PEACOCK

✳ HABITATIONS

Kings live in Palaces, and Pigs in sties,
And youth in Expectation. Youth is wise.
        HILAIRE BELLOC

✳ GRANDPA IS ASHAMED

A child need not be very clever
To learn that "Later, dear" means never.
        OGDEN NASH

✳

Base words are uttered only by the base
And can for such at once be understood,
But noble platitudes: ah, there's a case
Where the most careful scrutiny is needed
To tell a voice that's genuinely good
From one that's base but merely has succeeded.
        W. H. AUDEN

✴ International Copyright

In vain we call old notions fudge,
    And bend our conscience to our dealing;
The Ten Commandments will not budge,
    And stealing will continue stealing.

JAMES RUSSELL LOWELL

✴ Early Morning

"I try to look hard-boiled, but I
At heart am really very shy."
"I'm dreadfully self-conscious too;
I know I'm twice as shy as you."
"You're nowhere near so much as I."
"I am."
    "Like hell."
            "You lie."
                    "You lie."

MORRIS BISHOP

✴ Earth

"A planet doesn't explode of itself," said drily
The Martian astronomer, gazing off into the air—
"That they were able to do it is proof that highly
Intelligent beings must have been living there."

JOHN HALL WHEELOCK

✳ ARS POETICA

The goose that laid the golden egg
Died looking up its crotch
To find out how its sphincter worked.

Would you lay well? Don't watch.

X. J. KENNEDY

✳ ATHEIST

Poems are made by fools like me,
But only God can make a tree;

And only God who makes the tree
Also makes the fools like me.

But only fools like me, you see,
Can make a God, who makes a tree.

E. Y. HARBURG

✳ "HERMIT HOAR . . ."

Hermit hoar, in solemn cell,
 Wearing out life's evening gray,
Smite thy bosom, sage, and tell,
 What is bliss? and which the way?

Thus I spoke; and speaking sighed;
 Scarce repressed the starting tear;
When the smiling sage replied:
 "Come, my lad, and drink some beer."
   SAMUEL JOHNSON

✳

At lucky moments we seem on the brink
Of really saying what we think we think:
But, even then, an honest eye should wink.
   W. H. AUDEN

✳ ON THE VANITY OF
EARTHLY GREATNESS

The tusks that clashed in mighty brawls
Of mastodons, are billiard balls.

The sword of Charlemagne the Just
Is ferric oxide, known as rust.

The grizzly bear whose potent hug
Was feared by all, is now a rug.

Great Caesar's dead and on the shelf,
And I don't feel so well myself!

ARTHUR GUITERMAN

✳ EPIGRAM

The man who goes for Christian resignation
Will find his attitude his occupation.

J. V. CUNNINGHAM

✳ ELECTION REFLECTION

Each day into the upper air
Ascends the politician's prayer—
"Grant me the gift of swift retort
And keep the public memory short."

         M. KEEL JONES

✳ FATIGUE

I'm tired of Love: I'm still more tired of Rhyme.
But Money gives me pleasure all the time.

         HILAIRE BELLOC

✳

I'm beginning to lose patience
With my personal relations:
They are not deep,
And they are not cheap.

         W. H. AUDEN

✳ THE ADVERTISING AGENCY SONG

When your client's hopping mad,
Put his picture in the ad.
If he still should prove refractory
Add a picture of his factory.

         ANONYMOUS

✻ CONTEMPORARY NURSERY RHYME

The Queen was in the parlour,
    Polishing the grate;
The King was in the kitchen
    Washing up a plate;
The maid was in the garden
    Eating bread and honey,
Listening to the neighbours
    Offering her more money.
      (*London, 1940*)
      ANONYMOUS

When Statesmen gravely say "We must be realistic,"
The chances are they're weak and, therefore, pacifistic,
But when they speak of Principles, look out: perhaps
Their generals are already poring over maps.
    W. H. AUDEN

✻

Families, when a child is born,
Want it to be intelligent.
I, through intelligence having wrecked my whole life,
Only hope the baby will prove
Ignorant and stupid.
Then he will crown a tranquil life
By becoming a Cabinet Minister.
    TRANSLATED FROM THE CHINESE BY ARTHUR WALEY

✳ THE BRITISH JOURNALIST

You cannot hope
    To bribe or twist
(Thank God!) the British
    Journalist;
But, seeing what
    The man will do
Unbribed, there's no
    Occasion to.
      HUMBERT WOLFE

With what conviction the young man spoke
When he thought his nonsense rather a joke;
Now, when he doesn't doubt any more,
No one believes the booming old bore.
    W. H. AUDEN

He has observ'd the Golden Rule
Till he's become the Golden Fool.
    WILLIAM BLAKE (1757–1827)

✳ THE NET OF LAW

The net of law is spread so wide,
No sinner from its sweep may hide.

Its meshes are so fine and strong,
They take in every child of wrong.

O wonderous web of mystery!
Big fish alone escape from thee!

JAMES JEFFREY ROCHE

✳ A WORD OF ENCOURAGEMENT

O what a tangled web we weave
When first we practise to deceive!
But when we've practised quite a while
How vastly we improve our style!

J. R. POPE

✳ THE OPTIMIST

When the world is all against you;
When the race of life is run;
When the skies have turned to gray again—
Just say, "I've had me fun."
When the friends of yore all turn away
And sadness is the rule,
Just say, "The skies will turn again"
You silly, bloody fool!

ENGLISH MUSIC HALL RECITATION

✳ CHRISTMAS: 1924

"Peace upon earth!" was said. We sing it,
And pay a million priests to bring it.
After two thousand years of mass
We've got as far as poison-gas.

THOMAS HARDY

✳

Once for candy cook had stolen
X was punished by Papa;
When he asked where babies came from
He was lied to by Mamma.

Now the city streets are waiting
To mislead him, and he must
Keep an eye on aged beggars
Lest they strike him in disgust.

W. H. AUDEN

✳ EPISODE OF THE CHERRY TREE

An ill-advised
And foolish thing,
For us to harp
Upon this string;
The world will think
We're puzzled by
A patriot
Who would not lie.

MILDRED WESTON

IX *
THE THINGS
OF NATURE

✳ THE PRAYING MANTIS

From whence arrived the praying mantis?
From outer space, or lost Atlantis?
I glimpse the grim, green metal mug
That masks this pseudo-saintly bug,
Orthopterous, also carnivorous,
And faintly whisper, Lord deliver us.

OGDEN NASH

✳ BEETLE BEMUSED

With careful tread, through dim green-pillared halls,
Inch by long inch the purblind beetle crawls.
I watch, my forehead tickled by the grasses;
    Time passes.

Beetle, bemused, where every way's the same,
Turns and sets back along the road he came.
I roll upon my side and break my glasses;
    Time passes.

R. P. LISTER

✳ THE VIRUS

A Virus crouched upon the terrace
Watching for someone he might harass,
Then hurled himself with malice fierce
Upon a human, name of Pierce;
While Albert Pierce could but respond, "Hey,
Shoo!" and had him till next Monday.

CHRISTIAN MORGENSTERN
Translated from the German
by W. D. Snodgrass & Lore Segal

✳ TWEED AND TILL

Says Tweed to Till—
    "What gars ye rin sae still?"
Says Till to Tweed—
    "Though ye rin with speed
And I rin slaw,
    For ae man that ye droon
I droon twa."

ANONYMOUS

✴ THE OYSTER

The oyster's a confusing suitor;
It's masc., and fem., and even neuter.
At times it wonders, may what come,
Am I husband, wife, or chum.

OGDEN NASH

✴ DUCKS

Two white ducks waddle past my door
Moving fast:
They are needed somewhere!

ROBERT BLY

✴ TWO SMILES

The Smile of the Walrus is wild and distraught,
    And tinged with pale purples and greens,
Like the Smile of a Thinker who thinks a Great Thought
    And isn't quite sure what it means.

The Smile of the Goat has a meaning that few
    Will mistake, and explains in a measure
The Censor attending a risqué Review
    And combining Stern Duty with Pleasure.

OLIVER HERFORD

✳ THE BIRD

I love to hear the little bird
Into song by morning stirred,
Provided that he doesn't sing
Before my own awakening.
A bird that wakes a fellow up,
Should have been a buttercup.

SAMUEL HOFFENSTEIN

✳ THE ELEPHANT, OR THE FORCE OF HABIT

A tail behind, a trunk in front,
Complete the usual elephant.
The tail in front, the trunk behind,
Is what you very seldom find.

If you for specimens should hunt
With trunks behind and tails in front,
The hunt would occupy you long;
The force of habit is so strong.

A. E. HOUSMAN

✳ On a Horse and a Goat

Once, dreaming of eternal fire,
    I walked on hills aflame with gorse,
And saw a goat of great desire
    Paying addresses to a horse.

The horse was shocked, and so was I,
    Until I saw, above this scene,
The sweet and sempiternal sky,
    Smiling, seraphic, and serene.

I cannot say I understood
    How things so pure could be so coarse;
But, still, I knew the goat was good—
    Though not so virtuous as the horse.

      R. P. LISTER

✳ Starlings

Overnight my garden is Yoknapatawpha.
The Snopeses have taken possession. Shoddily-spruce
in their handmedown tweeds, conferring cacophonously
in dry-axle falsettos, they blackguard their way to the
    feeder.
The gentry cringe and retreat: yes, even the bluejay,
a Sartoris if ever I knew one. Not yet having learned,
as most of us learn, to endure the boor and the sharper,
he squalls patrician goddamits from the magnolia.

    TED OLSON

✳ Wanted

Can anyone lend me two twelve-pound rats?
I want to rid my house of cats.

SHEL SILVERSTEIN

✳ Epitaph for a
Lighthouse-Keeper's Horse

Here lies the lighthouse-keeper's horse,
Which was not ridden much, of course;
How patiently it waited for
The lighthouse-keeper's leave on shore!

"Beachcomber"
(J. B. MORTON)

The parrot and the carrot we may easily confound,
They're very much alike in looks and similar in sound;
We recognize the parrot by his clear articulation,
For carrots are unable to engage in conversation.

ROBERT W. WOOD

✻ THE GRACKLE

The grackle's voice is less than mellow,
His heart is black, his eye is yellow,
He bullies more attractive birds
With hoodlum deeds and vulgar words,
And should a human interfere,
Attacks that human in the rear.
I cannot help but deem the grackle
An ornithological debacle.

OGDEN NASH

✻ A PENGUIN

The Pen-guin sits upon the shore
And loves the lit-tle fish to bore;
He has one en-er-va-ting joke
That would a very Saint provoke:
"The *Pen*-guin's might-i-er than the *Sword*-fish";
He tells this dai-ly to the bored fish,
Un-til they are so weak, they float
With-out re-sis-tance down his throat.

OLIVER HERFORD

❋ The Day of the Crucifixion

Hunters were oot on a Scottish hill
A'e day when the sun stude suddenly still
At noon and turned the color o' port
A perfect nuisance, spoilin' their sport.
Syne it gaed pitch black a'thegither.
Isn't that juist like oor Scottish weather!
                HUGH MACDIARMID

❋ The Bat

Myself, I rather like the bat,
It's not a mouse, it's not a rat.
It has no feathers, yet has wings,
It's quite inaudible when it sings.
It zigzags through the evening air
And never lands on ladies' hair,
A fact of which men spend their lives
Attempting to convince their wives.
                OGDEN NASH

✳ ON BECOMING MAN

I well remember how the race began.
 I was, as I recall, a kind of fish,
But some strange fancy told me to be man.
 The course of things responded to my wish.

And shortly I was sprouting arms and legs,
 And straightening out my unaccustomed spine.
True to my vow, I gave up laying eggs;
 I hunted sometimes, when the day was fine.

I took the dog for friend, and tamed the cow,
 And learned to write, despite the mental strain,
And never told my friends and neighbors how
 I sometimes longed to be a fish again.

   R. P. LISTER

✳ MAX SCHLING, MAX SCHLING, LEND ME YOUR GREEN THUMB

A travelogue of Flowery Catalogues

Bobolink!
Bobolink!
Spink!
Spank!
Spink!
Bobbink!
Atkink!
Sprink!

Burpee.
OGDEN NASH

X *
EPIGRAMS

✳ What Is an Epigram?

What is an epigram? A dwarfish whole;
Its body brevity and wit its soul.
SAMUEL TAYLOR COLERIDGE

✳ Epigram

I had gone broke, and got set to come back,
And lost, on a hot day and a fast track,
On a long shot at long odds, a black mare
By Hatred out of Envy by Despair.
J. V. CUNNINGHAM

✳ Afterthought

Earth labored, and lo! Man lay in her lap—
She murmured "Homo" . . . and then added "Sap!"
JUSTIN RICHARDSON

✳ Epigram

The arctic raven tracks the caribou,
    Gorges its ordure for life's bitter sake.
    Before you say that's more than you would do,
Ask yourself whether you've as much at stake.
RAYMOND WILSON

*

Private faces in public places
Are wiser and nicer
Than public faces in private places.
W. H. AUDEN

* ON SCOTLAND

Had Cain been Scot, God would have changed his doom;
Nor forced him wander, but confined him home.
JOHN CLEVELAND (1631–1658)

* ON A PROUD FELLOW

Jack his own merit sees: this gives him pride,
That he sees more than all the world beside.
ANONYMOUS
FROM *Epigrams in Distich*, 1740

* THE MISTAKEN RESOLVE

Thou swear'st thou'lt drink no more; kind heaven
   send
Me such a cook or coachman, but no friend.
MARTIAL
FROM *A Collection of Epigrams*, 1727

✳ ON A SUNDIAL

I am a sundial, and I make a botch
Of what is done far better by a watch.
      HILAIRE BELLOC

✳ GREAT THINGS

Great things are done when Men & Mountains meet;
This is not done by Jostling in the Street.
      WILLIAM BLAKE

✳ REVENGE

Lie on! while my revenge shall be,
To speak the very truth of thee.
      LORD NUGENT (1702–1788)

✳

Twelve hundred million men are spread
    About this Earth, and I and You
Wonder, when You and I are dead
    "What will those luckless millions do?"
      RUDYARD KIPLING

❋ QUESTION AND ANSWER

What is so rare as a day in June?
Decent behavior
From a popular savior.

SAMUEL HOFFENSTEIN

❋

He drank strong waters and his speech was coarse;
He purchased raiment and forbore to pay;
He stuck a trusting junior with a horse,
And won gymkhanas in a doubtful way.
Then, 'twixt a vice and folly, turned aside
To do good deeds and straight to cloak them, lied.

RUDYARD KIPLING

❋ EPIGRAM

I married in my youth a wife.
She was my own, my very first.
She gave me the best years of her life.
I hope nobody gets the worst.

J. V. CUNNINGHAM

✳ APOCRYPHA

Great Yahweh fingered through His Bible,
Thought on it, and filed suit for libel.
> X. J. KENNEDY

✳

Her whole Life is an Epigram, smart, smooth, & neatly
    pen'd,
Platted quite neat to catch applause with a sliding noose
    at the end.
> WILLIAM BLAKE

✳ COMMON FORM

If any question why we died,
Tell them, because our fathers lied.
> RUDYARD KIPLING

✳ ON THE PHRASE, "TO KILL TIME"

There's scarce a point whereon mankind agree
So well, as in their boast of killing time:
I boast of nothing, but, when I've a mind,
I think I can be even with mankind.
> VOLTAIRE (1694–1778)

✳ VANITY

Once in a saintly passion
    I cried with desperate grief,
O Lord, my heart is black with guile,
    Of sinners I am chief.
Then stooped my guardian angel
    And whispered from behind,
"Vanity, my little man,
    You're nothing of the kind."
      JAMES THOMSON (B.V.)

✳ THE POWER OF TIME

If neither brass nor marble can withstand
The mortal force of Time's destructive hand;
If mountains sink to vales, if cities die,
And lessening rivers mourn their fountains dry;
When my old cassock (said a Welsh divine)
Is out at elbows, why should I repine?
      JONATHAN SWIFT (1667–1745)

PLAYS

Alas, how soon the hours are over
Counted us out to play the lover!
And how much narrower is the stage
Allotted us to play the sage!

But when we play the fool, how wide
The theater expands! beside,
How long the audience sits before us!
How many prompters! what a chorus!
                    WALTER SAVAGE LANDOR

INVENTIONS

All the inventions that the world contains,
Were not by reason first found out, nor brains;
But pass for theirs who had the luck to light
Upon them by mistake or oversight.
                    SAMUEL BUTLER

##

'Tis an old Maxim in the Schools,
That Vanity's the Food of Fools;
Yet now and then your Men of Wit
Will condescend to take a bit.
                    JONATHAN SWIFT

The only Man that e'er I knew
Who did not make me almost spew
Was Fuseli: he was both Turk & Jew—
And so, dear Christian Friends, how do you do?

WILLIAM BLAKE

XI *
SHORT CLASSICS

❋ Wishes of an Elderly Man

Wished at a Garden Party, June, 1914

I wish I loved the Human Race;
I wish I loved its silly face;
I wish I liked the way it walks;
I wish I liked the way it talks;
And when I'm introduced to one
I wish I thought *What Jolly Fun!*

      SIR WALTER RALEIGH

❋ Manila

Oh, dewy was the morning, upon the first of May,
And Dewey was the admiral, down in Manila Bay;
And dewy were the Regent's eyes, them royal orbs of blue,
And do we feel discouraged? We do not think we do!

      EUGENE F. WARE

❋ A True Maid

No, no; for my virginity,
When I lose that, says Rose, I'll die:
Behind the elms, last night, cried Dick,
Rose, were you not extremely sick?

      MATTHEW PRIOR (1664–1721)

✳ COLOGNE

In Cologne, a town of monks and bones,
And pavements fanged with murderous stones
And rags, and hags, and hideous wenches;
I counted two and seventy stenches,
All well defined, and several stinks!
Ye Nymphs that reign o'er sewers and sinks,
The river Rhine, it is well known,
Doth wash your city of Cologne;
But tell me, Nymphs, what power divine
Shall henceforth wash the river Rhine?

SAMUEL TAYLOR COLERIDGE

✳ TO THE CUCKOO

O Cuckoo! shall I call thee Bird,
  Or but a wandering Voice?

W. WORDSWORTH

✳

State the alternative preferred
With reasons for your choice.

F. H. TOWNSEND

✻ To Be Continued

Said Opie Read to E. P. Roe,
"How do you like Gaboriau?"
"I like him very much indeed,"
Said E. P. Roe to Opie Read.
JULIAN STREET and JAMES MONTGOMERY FLAGG

✻ On "Who Wrote Icon Basilike"
by Dr. Christopher Wordsworth,
Master of Trinity

Who wrote *Who wrote Icon Basilike?*
I, said the Master of Trinity,
With my small ability,
I wrote *Who wrote Icon Basilike?*
BENJAMIN HALL KENNEDY

✻ The Great Auk's Ghost

The Great Auk's ghost rose on one leg,
Sighed thrice and three times winkt,
And turned and poached a phantom egg
And muttered, "I'm extinct."
RALPH HODGSON

✳ BOBBY'S FIRST POEM

Itt rely is ridikkelus
how uncle Charley tikkles us
at eester and at mikklemus
upon the nursry floor.

and rubbs our chins and bites our ears
like firty-fousand poler bares
and roars like lyons down the stares
and won't play enny more.

NORMAN GALE

✳ MISS TWYE

Miss Twye was soaping her breasts in her bath
When she heard behind her a meaning laugh
And to her amazement she discovered
A wicked man in the bathroom cupboard.

GAVIN EWART

✳ THE RAIN IT RAINETH

The rain it raineth on the just
    And also on the unjust fella;
But chiefly on the just, because
    The unjust steals the just's umbrella.

LORD BOWEN

CROMEK

A petty sneaking knave I knew—
O Mr. Cromek, how do ye do?
WILLIAM BLAKE

Hark the Herald Angels sing,
Beecham's pills are just the thing!
Two for a woman, one for a child,
Peace on earth and mercy mild!
SIR THOMAS BEECHAM
(composed, as a teenager, for his father)

*

Would you like to sin
With Elinor Glyn
On a tiger skin?

Or would you prefer
To err with her
On some other fur?
ANONYMOUS
(inspired by her 1907 then-shocking novel Three
Weeks)

✳

I was playing golf that day
    When the Germans landed.
All our soldiers ran away,
    All our ships were stranded.
Such were my surprise and shame
They almost put me off my game.✳
      ANONYMOUS

✳

I am the great Professor Jowett:
What there is to know, I know it.
I am the Master of Balliol College,
And what I don't know isn't knowledge.
      ANONYMOUS

✳ COMMUTER

Commuter—one who spends his life
In riding to and from his wife;
A man who shaves and takes a train
And then rides back to shave again.
      E. B. WHITE

✳ Popular in London early in World War I; aimed at Arthur Balfour, First Lord of the Admiralty.

✳ On an Imaginary Journey to the Continent

I went to Frankfort and got drunk
With that most learned professor—Brunck;
I went to Worts, and got more drunken,
With that more learned professor—Runchen.

RICHARD PORSON (1759–1808)

✳ Abdication Street Song

Hark the herald angels sing
"Mrs. Simpson's pinched our King."

ANONYMOUS

✳ An Expostulation

When late I attempted your pity to move,
    What made you so deaf to my prayers?
Perhaps it was right to dissemble your love,
    But—why did you kick me down stairs?

ISAAC BICKERSTAFF (1735–1812?)

XII *
FARTHER OUT

✳ Banana

a phallus going around a corner

carefully

ADRIAN MITCHELL

✳ Invitation

Come in, she said, but
I couldn't come in. I
had mud on my shoes.

Take off your shoes, she said,
but I couldn't do that.
I had holes in my stockings.

Take off your stockings, she said,
but I couldn't do that either.
I had holes in my feet
from the nails.

VICTOR CONTOSKI

✳ "I Am Almost Asleep"

I am almost asleep
with your poems on my chest,

Apollinaire

I am almost asleep,
but I feel a transfusion of fine little letters
dripping slantwise into my side.
            ELDON GRIER

✳ The Guest

Every day now, since my wife told me to cease from
            writing poems
I've been treating myself to these American prunes;
and she has come to see me, whose breasts
are "so moist and tender, you can eat them like candy."
            PENTTI SAARIKOSKI
            (*translated from the Finnish by Anselm Hollo*)

✳ The King of Sunshine

In the forest there
a man is painting some trees yellow.
He screeches once in a while.
A thoughtful fellow,
he seems odd in the forest.
            MICHAEL SILVERTON

✳ A Chasm

I notified the Chasm Inspector about
a chasm I happened upon
on my way home from my place of employment.
He was pleased indeed!
He rewarded me with a box of yodel spume
& a ride on his sunset machine.

MICHAEL SILVERTON

✳

So long as Time & Space are the stars
you're the zero-hero the merest
birthday cake a thread of gunk
a peanut salesman
a nothing

except to me. I think you're great.

MICHAEL SILVERTON

✳ Column A

It was strange when I fell to the bottom of Column A
It made me feel languid
It made me feel like letting off some air for decoration

MICHAEL SILVERTON

❋ Neckwear

May I borrow your handpainted cravat?
I want to garrote myself with it with
a view to being recalled as one
of Fashion's tragic figures.
MICHAEL SILVERTON

❋ Goosepimples

crowdpleasers
coming down the aisles
of my arms and legs:

crowds of the pleased
stand up and clap
COLEMAN BARKS

❋ Semen

thousands
of weird little figurines
carved out of soap

suddenly come alive
and jabber like
foreigners
COLEMAN BARKS

✳ Downy Hair in the Shape of a Flame Moving Up the Stomach and Ending at the Solar Plexus

anything this
recognizable

should have
a name:

COLEMAN BARKS

✳ The Geriatric Whore

The geriatric whore
Puts flowers in all the floppy old peters
And lays a spoonful of semen on each man's belly
While he sleeps

It's the greatest
Old folks home in the country.

PETE WINSLOW

✳ The Dream Motorcycle

I rode a dream motorcycle
Through a rural village
There was a blacksmith's shop
But my dream became phallic at the wrong time
And startled all the horses
I wasn't invited back.

PETE WINSLOW

✳ The Mad Rapist of
Calaveras County

The mad rapist of Calaveras County
Made love to the jumping frog
And all through the night you could hear them shout
"Let me go you fool!" and "Hot dog!"

PETE WINSLOW

✷ DISCLAIMER OF PREJUDICE

It's no use having good taste in Chicago.
You've got to change your city before it means anything.
This is not racial prejudice.
It's not your skin or your religion.
It's the city.
    II
I've never been on State Street, Chicago,
And I've never dreamed of being on it.
All I've done is to read about people who have been on it
      and near it.
And I pitied them, always, a little.
    III
So it's not your race,
Or your skin or your religion.
It's the city.

      ELI SIEGEL

* INDEX OF AUTHORS

(continued from copyright page)

Kevin Crossley-Holland for "Riddle" from *TLS*, copyright © 1968 by Kevin Crossley-Holland.

Definition Press for "Disclaimer of Prejudice" by Eli Siegel, from *Hail, American Development;* copyright © 1968.

The Literary Trustees of Walter de la Mare and The Society of Authors as their representative for "The Bards" by Walter de la Mare.

The Dial Press for "Early Morning" and "The Naughty Preposition" from *A Bowl of Bishop,* copyright 1954 by Morris Bishop and used by permission of the publisher, The Dial Press, Inc. "The Naughty Preposition" originally published in *The New Yorker.*

Dennis Dobson, Ltd. for "A thousand hairy savages" from *Silly Verse for Kids,* by Spike Milligan; used by permission of Dennis Dobson, Ltd.

Dodd, Mead & Company for "The Sceptic" by Robert Service from *The Collected Poems of Robert Service;* copyright 1912 by Dodd, Mead & Company, Inc.; copyright renewed 1939 by Robert Service. Reprinted by permission of Dodd, Mead & Company, Inc.

Doubleday & Company for "Ars Poetica" by X. J. Kennedy from the book *Nude Descending a Staircase;* copyright © 1961 by X. J. Kennedy; reprinted by permission of Doubleday & Company, Inc.

Doubleday & Company for "Common Form" by Rudyard Kipling, from *Rudyard Kipling's Verse,* copyright 1919 by Rudyard Kipling. Reprinted by permission of Mrs. George Bambridge and Doubleday & Company, Inc.

E. P. Dutton & Company for "Doctor Emmanuel," from *The Wandering Moon* by James Reeves. Published in 1960 by E. P. Dutton & Co., Inc., and reprinted with their permission.

Colin Ellis for "Spaniel's Sermon" from *Mournful Numbers;* reprinted by permission of the author.

Gavin Ewart for "Miss Twye"; copyright by Gavin Ewart; reprinted by permission of the the author.

David Higham Associates, Ltd. for "Apologia" by Herbert Farjeon from *Nine Sharp and Earlier.* Reprinted by permission.

William Heinemann Ltd. for "On the Imprint of the First Edition of 'The Works of Max Beerbohm' " from *Max in Verse,* published by The Stephen Greene Press.

William Heinemann Ltd. for "Lines on a Certain Friend's Remarkable Faculty for Swift Generalisation" from *Max in Verse,* by Max Beerbohm, published by The Stephen Greene Press. Reprinted by permission.

Eldon Grier for "I am Almost Asleep" from *A Friction of Lights,* by Eldon Grier, published by Contact Press; copyright © by Eldon Grier; reprinted by permission of the author.

Geoffrey Grigson for "Lecture Note: Elizabethan Period" from *A Skull in Salop* by Geoffrey Grigson; copyright © by Geoffrey Grigson; reprinted by permission of the author.

Grossman Publishers for "Atheist" by E. Y. Harburg from *Rhymes for the Irreverent;* reprinted by permission.

Grove Press, Inc. for "Variations on a Theme" by William Carlos Williams from *Thank You and Other Poems,* by Kenneth Koch; copyright © 1962 by Kenneth Koch; reprinted by permission of Grove Press, Inc.

Mrs. Arthur Guiterman for "On the Vanity of Earthly Greatness" from *Gaily the Troubadour* by Arthur Guiterman, published by Dutton in 1936; copyright 1936 by E. P. Dutton & Co.; copyright © renewed in 1964 by Mrs. Arthur Guiterman.

Harcourt, Brace & World for "Token" from *Animosities,* by Peggy Bacon; copyright 1931 by Harcourt, Brace & World, Inc., copyright © renewed in 1959 by Peggy Bacon and reprinted by permission of the publishers.

Harper & Row for "Commuter" from *The Lady Is Cold,* by E. B. White; copyright 1925 by E. B. White; reprinted by permission of the publishers; originally appeared in *The New Yorker.*

Harper & Row for "The Newlyweds" from *The Carpentered Hen and Other Tame Creatures* by John Updike; copyright © 1955 by John Updike; reprinted by permission of the publishers; originally appeared in *The New Yorker.*

Piet Hein for "Lilac Time" from *Grooks*, by Piet Hein; copyright © 1969 by Piet Hein; reprinted by permission of Doubleday & Co.

David Hoffenstein for "Question and Answer" from *Pencil in the Air* by Samuel Hoffenstein; copyright © by David Hoffenstein.

A. D. Hope for "The pronunciation of Erse . . ."; reprinted by permission of the author.

R. G. Howarth for "Memoir" from *Cats of Mine;* copyright © 1963 by R. G. Howarth.

X. J. Kennedy for "To Someone Who Insisted I Look Someone Up" and "Apocrypha" by X. J. Kennedy; reprinted by permission of the author.

Kenneth Koch for "Mending Sump." Reprinted by permission.

Tuli Kupferberg for "I saw your hinee"; copyright by *Swing #3* and Lenore Jaffe.

Seymour Lawrence Books for "Edmund Clerihew Bentley" and "William Penn" from *Mr. Smith & Other Nonsense* by William Jay Smith; copyright © 1968 by William Jay Smith; copyright © 1968 by Don Bolognese. A Seymour Lawrence Book/Delacorte Press. Reprinted by permission.

Little, Brown and Company for "Grandpa Is Ashamed" from *There's Always Another Windmill* by Ogden Nash; copyright © 1966 by Ogden Nash; reprinted by permission of Little, Brown and Company.

Little, Brown and Company for "The Lama," "The Purist," "The Praying Mantis," "Max Schling, Max Schling . . . ," "The Oyster," "The Grackle," and "The Bat," from *Verses From 1929*, by Ogden Nash. "The Bat," copyright 1952 by Ogden Nash; "The Grackle," copyright 1942 by The Curtis Publishing Co.; "The Lama," copyright 1931 by Ogden Nash; "Max Schling, Max Schling . . . ," copyright 1952 by Ogden Nash; "The Oyster," copyright 1931 by Ogden Nash; "The Purist," copyright 1935 by The Curtis Publishing Co.; "The Praying Mantis," copyright © 1956 by Ogden Nash, first appeared in *The New Yorker*. Reprinted by permission of Little, Brown and Company.

Liveright Publishing Corporation for "The Bird" from *Treasury of Humorous Verse* by Samuel Hoffenstein; copyright 1946 by Liveright Publishing Corp. Reprinted by permission of Liveright Publishers.

McClelland and Stewart Ltd. for "Hostia" from *The Swinging Flesh* by Irving Layton and "Misunderstanding" by Irving Layton; reprinted by permission of The Canadian Publishers, McClelland and Stewart Ltd., Toronto.

The Macmillan Company for "Christmas: 1924" from *Winter Woods* by Thomas Hardy, copyright 1928 by Florence E. Hardy and Sydney Cockerell; "The Great Auk's Ghost" from *Poems* by Ralph Hodgson; copyright 1917 by The Macmillan Company, renewed in 1945 by Ralph Hodgson; "The Day of the Crucifixion" from *Collected Poems* by Hugh MacDiarmid, copyright © 1948, 1962 by Murray Christopher Grieve; "To a Poet Who Would Have Me Praise Certain Bad Poets" from *Collected Poems* by William Butler Yeats; copyright 1912 by The Macmillan Company, renewed 1940 by Bertha Georgie Yeats. All of the above are reprinted by permission of The Macmillan Company.

Harold Matson Company for "Beetle Bemused" and "On a Horse and a Goat" by R. P. Lister; copyright by R. P. Lister; reprinted by permission of Harold Matson Co., Inc.

Adrian Mitchell for "Telegram One." Reprinted by permission.

John Bingham Morton for "Beachcomber" and "On Sir Henry Ferrett, M.P." from *By the Way* by J. B. Morton.

The Nation for "Love" by Gerald Jonas and "Dinah" by A. R. Ammons, published in *The Nation*.

The *New Statesman* for "The Bedbug" by Tony Harrison, "Miniskirt" by Anthony Mundy, and "Albert Dürer" by Leslie W. Nicholls; reprinted by permission.

Richard O'Connell for "Sidewalk Orgy" by Richard O'Connell, from *Atlantic Monthly*; reprinted by permission of the author.

Ted Olson (Theodore B. Olson) for "Starlings" from *Atlantic Monthly*; reprinted by permission of the author.

Oxford University Press for "The Bulge" by George Johnston and "Eurynome" by Jay MacPherson from *The Boatman*; reprinted by permission of the publishers.

Penguin Books for "To the Noble Woman of Llanarth Hall" by Evan Thomas, from *The Penguin Book of Welsh Verse*, translated and edited by Anthony Conran. Reprinted by permission of Penguin Books.

A. D. Peters & Co. for "Epitaph for a Lighthousekeeper's Horse" and "Epitaph on a Warthog" from *Morton's Folly* by J. B. Morton published by Sheed & Ward Ltd. Reprinted by permission of A. D. Peters & Co.

A. D. Peters & Co. for "Now We Are Sick" from *The Best of Beachcomber* by J. B. Morton, published by William Heinemann Ltd. Reprinted by permission of A. D. Peters & Co.

A. D. Peters & Co. for "Fatigue," "Habitations," "On a Politician," "On a Sundial," "On Noman," "On Two Ministers of State," and "On Lady Poltragrue," from *Sonnets and Verse* by Hilaire Belloc, published by Gerald Duckworth & Co. Ltd. Reprinted by permission of A. D. Peters & Co.

Random House for excerpts from *Collected Shorter Poems 1927-1957* by W. H. Auden; copyright © 1966 by W. H. Auden. Reprinted by permission of Random House, Inc.

Random House for "The Curse" and "Epitaph" from *Complete Works of J. M. Synge*; copyright 1909 and renewed 1936 by Edward Synge and Francis Edmund Stephens. Reprinted by permission of Random House, Inc.

Random House for "The Voice of Experience" by Goethe from *Twenty German Poets*, translated by Walter Kaufman; copyright © 1962 by Random House, Inc. Reprinted by permission.

Random House for "At lucky moments we are on the brink . . ." from *About the House* by W. H. Auden. Reprinted by permission of Random House, Inc.

Mr. Justin Richardson for "Afterthought," "High-Life Low-Down," "Garlic" and "Red Wine," by Justin Richardson. Reprinted by permission of the author.

Alan Ross Ltd. for "Professor Drinking Wine" by Alasdair Clayre, from *London Magazine Poems*, and "Nymphs and Satyrs" by Gavin Ewart from *The Deceptive Grin of the Gravel Porters*; copyright © *London Magazine*. Reprinted by permission of Alan Ross Ltd.

The Ben Roth Agency for thirteen poems from *Punch*; copyright © *Punch*.

Rutgers University Press for "Visiting Poet" from *Flesh and Bone* by John Frederick Nims. Reprinted by permission of Rutgers University Press.

Stevie Smith for "Miss Snooks" from *Selected Poems*, published by Longmans Green & Co. Ltd. Reprinted by permission of the author.

Charles Scribner's Sons for "The Elephant, or the Force of Habit" and "Hallelujah" by A. E. Housman from *My Brother, A. E. Housman*, by Laurence Housman; copyright 1937, 1938 by Laurence Housman; renewal copyright © 1965, 1966 by Lloyds Bank Ltd. Reprinted by permission of Charles Scribner's Sons.

Charles Scribner's Sons for "Earth" from *The Gardener and Other Poems* by John Hall Wheelock; copyright © 1960 by John Hall Wheelock. Reprinted by permission of Charles Scribner's Sons.

Shel Silverstein for "Wanted" and "My Invention" by Shel Silverstein; reprinted by permission of the author.

Michael Silverton for "A Chasm," "Column A," "The King of Sunshine," "Neckwear," "So long as Time and Space are the Stars" by Michael Silverton; reprinted by permission of the author.

Simon and Schuster for selections from *Quake, Quake, Quake* by Paul Dehn; copyright © 1961 by Paul Dehn. Reprinted by permission of Simon and Schuster.

A. J. M. Smith for "The Taste of Space."

George Starbuck for "Averell Harriman," "Samuel Eliot Morison," "Cesare Borgia," "President Johnson," "Agatha Christie," and "J. Alfred Prufrock," by George Starbuck; copyright © 1969 by George Starbuck.

The Swallow Press for "Epigrams" by J. V. Cunningham from *The Exclusions of a Rhyme*, Swallow Press, Chicago; copyright © 1960.

The Swallow Press for "Number 8" by J. V. Cunningham from *To What Strangers, What Welcome*, Swallow Press, Chicago; copyright © 1964.

The Swallow Press for "The Guest" by Pentti Saarikiski from *Helsinki,* Anselm Hollo, translator; Swallow Press, Chicago; copyright © 1967.

Tennessee Poetry Journal for "Goosepimples," "Downy hair in the shape of a flame . . ." and "Semen" by Coleman Parks from Fall issue; copyright © 1968 by Tennessee Poetry Journal.

University of Michigan Press for "The Virus" from *Gallows Songs,* by Christian Morgenstern, translated by W. D. Snodgrass and Lore Segal; copyright © 1967 by University of Michigan.

University of Washington Press for "Specialist" by Theodore Roethke from *Selected Letters of Theodore Roethke;* copyright by Beatrice Roethke and published by University of Washington Press.

The Viking Press for "It's No Good!" from *The Complete Poems of D. H. Lawrence,* Volume I, edited by Vivian de Sola Pinto and F. Warren Roberts; copyright 1929 by Frieda Lawrence Ravagli; all rights reserved; reprinted by permission of The Viking Press, Inc.

T. Werner Laurie Ltd. for 7 clerihews from *Clerihews Complete,* by E. C. Bentley: "The Art of Biography," "Sir Christopher Wren," "George the Third," "The Great Emperor Otto," "Geoffrey Chaucer," "Susaddah! Exclaimed Ibsen," and "The Digestion of Milton." Reprinted by permission of the publishers, T. Werner Laurie Ltd.

Raymond Wilson for "Epigram" copyright © by Raymond Wilson; reprinted by permission of the author.

Pete Winslow for "The Geriatric Whore," "The Dream Motorcycle," and "The Mad Rapist of Calaveras County," from *Monster Cookies,* copyright © 1967 by Pete Winslow. "The Dream Motorcycle" appeared in Kirby Congdon's *Magazine 3.*

Ann Wolfe for "The British Journalist" from *The Uncelestial City* by Humbert Wolfe; reprinted by permission of Miss Ann Wolfe.